TIMELINE *of*
WORLD WAR I

By Charlie Samuels

Please visit our website, www.garethstevens.com. For a free color catalog of all our high-quality books, call toll free 1-800-542-2595 or fax 1-877-542-2596.

Library of Congress Cataloging-in-Publication Data
Samuels, Charlie, 1961-
Timeline of World War I / Charlie Samuels.
    p. cm.— (Americans at war : a Gareth Stevens timeline series)
Includes bibliographical references and index.
ISBN 978-1-4339-5928-8 (pbk.)
ISBN 978-1-4339-5929-5 (6-pack)
ISBN 978-1-4339-5926-4 (library binding)
1. World War, 1914-1918—Campaigns—Juvenile literature. 2. World War, 1914-1918—Campaigns—Chronology—Juvenile literature. 3. World War, 1914-1918—Juvenile literature. 4. World War, 1914-1918—Chronology—Juvenile literature. I. Title. II. Title: Timeline of World War 1. III. Title: Timeline of World War One.
D522.7.S26 2011
940.4—dc22
                                                                                    2010054458

Published in 2012 by
Gareth Stevens Publishing
111 East 14th Street, Suite 349
New York, NY 10003

© 2012 Brown Bear Books Limited

For Brown Bear Books:
Editorial Director: Lindsey Lowe
Managing Editor: Tim Cooke
Children's Publisher: Anne O'Daly
Art Director: Jeni Child
Designer: Karen Perry
Picture Manager: Sophie Mortimer
Production Director: Alastair Gourlay

Picture Credits:
Front Cover: Robert Hunt Library

All photographs: Robert Hunt Library
All Artworks © Brown Bear Books Limited

Manufactured in the United States of America
1 2 3 4 5 6 7 8 9 12 11 10

CPSIA compliance information: Batch #BRS11GS: For further information contact Gareth Stevens, New York, New York at 1-800-542-2595.

Contents

Introduction 4

Causes of the War 6

The Outbreak of War 10

The Eastern Front 14

Failure at Gallipoli 18

The War at Sea 22

The Struggle at Verdun 26

Slaughter on the Somme 30

A Pivotal Year 34

Germany's Last Gamble 38

US Pressure Counts 42

Glossary 46

Further Reading 47

Index 48

Introduction

For those who lived through it, the conflict that engulfed much of the world from 1914 to 1918 was known as "The Great War" or "The War to End War."

World War I was fought on a previously unimaginable scale. More than 35 million people died. The image of hundreds of thousands of men dying for little gain in the mud of the Western Front became a lasting symbol of the futility of war.

The Course of the War

The causes of the war lay in rivalries among Europe's great powers. The assassination of an Austrian archduke in 1914 triggered a chain reaction that rapidly brought millions of men into military service. The Germans raced to defeat their French neighbors before turning to face the Russians; the failure of their plan left them fighting on two fronts. In the west, the armies dug lines of trenches that would barely move for five years, despite enormous loss of life. Aircraft clashed in dogfights above the trenches, while Zeppelin airships launched the first air raids on civilians. An attempt by the Allies (Britain and its empire, France, and Russia) to open a new front in Turkey failed at Gallipoli. At sea, warships clashed rarely, but one intervention—the sinking of the liner *Lusitania* by a German submarine—changed the course of the war by drawing in the United States. The arrival of US forces would finally break the deadlock on the Western Front and open the way to Allied victory.

About This Book

This book contains two types of timelines. Along the bottom of the pages is a timeline that covers the whole period. It lists key events and developments, color coded to indicate the Western Front, Eastern Front, and other theaters of the war. Each chapter also has its own timeline, which runs vertically down the sides of the pages. This timeline gives more specific details about the particular subject of the chapter.

The crew of a British 12-inch (30 cm) howitzer prepares to open fire at the start of the Battle of Arras in April 1917. ↓

Causes of the War

In 1914, many European leaders wanted their countries to be strong and rich. They were prepared to take from other countries and fight wars to achieve their aims.

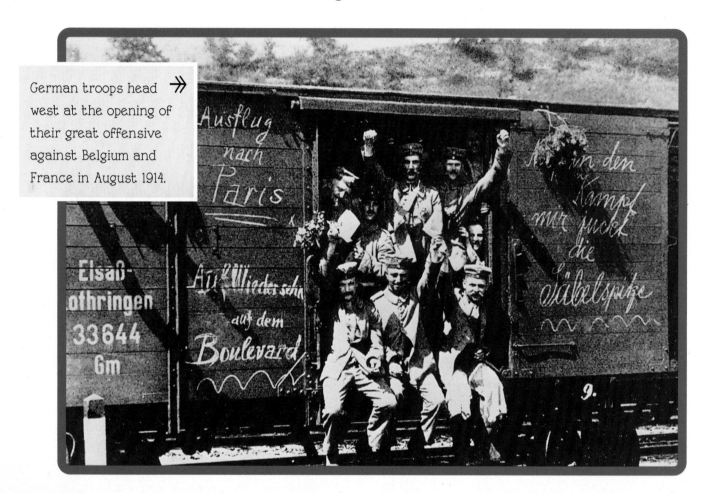

German troops head ➔ west at the opening of their great offensive against Belgium and France in August 1914.

Timeline
1914
June–July

June

KEY:

 Western Front

Eastern Front

 Other fronts

June 28 Bosnia Archduke Franz Ferdinand and his wife are assassinated by a Serb during a visit to Sarajevo.

Although it soon involved countries and people from virtually every continent on Earth, World War I began as a European conflict. The United States, the only major world power outside Europe, did not join the war until 1917.

Powerful European Rivals

The map of Europe in 1914 was very different from that of today. There were five "great powers": Germany, Austria-Hungary, France, Russia, and Britain. They had formed two opposing alliances: Austria-Hungary and Germany (the Central powers) on one side; on the other, Britain, France, and Russia, known as the Entente (or Allies). The powers were economic rivals; many were carving out overseas empires, and the majority had potentially huge armies supplied by vast armament industries. Such factors caused great suspicion between the two power blocs. Their rivalries needed just one event to drag them into physical conflict.

Timeline

June 28, 1914 Franz Ferdinand, heir to the throne of the Austro-Hungarian Empire, is assassinated in Sarajevo, the capital of Bosnia, by a Serb.

July 25, 1914 Serbia rejects Austro-Hungarian demands that Serbia become part of their empire; the Austrians prepare for war with Serbia, which Russia is committed to protect.

August 1, 1914 Germany, an ally of Austria-Hungary, declares war on Russia.

August 3, 1914 Germany declares war on France, an ally of Russia.

August 4, 1914 Great Britain and its empire declare war on the Central powers.

← A Bosnian official greets Archduke Franz Ferdinand shortly before his assassination.

July 23 Austria-Hungary
The Austro-Hungarians issue an ultimatum to Serbia that would end Serbia's existence as an independent state.

July 31 Germany
Germany informs Russia that it must halt its mobilization.

July

July 25 Serbia Serbia rejects the Austro-Hungarian ultimatum; Russian Czar Nicholas II mobilizes troops ready to protect Serbia.

July 29 Germany
Germany begins to mobilize its High Seas Fleet.

Germany's War Plans

In 1914, the German army was the most powerful in Europe. Count Alfred von Schlieffen, a former chief of staff, had come up with the plan on which German strategy was based in 1914. It relied on railroads to move troops around rapidly. However, war can rarely be exactly planned or predicted. Events soon proved that Schlieffen's "war by timetable" was impossible.

The Schlieffen Plan

Germany's military leaders feared a war on two fronts, simultaneously fighting the Russians and the French. They believed that the Russians would take longer to mobilize their armies. Count Alfred von Schlieffen therefore devised a plan to be followed if war began: Germany would quickly defeat France before turning to face Russia. The strategy meant that, in the event of war, the German army would immediately begin an attack on France.

War Begins

In 1914, Austria-Hungary, Germany, and Russia became involved in a quarrel over Serbia, a small country friendly to Russia. After a member of Austria-Hungary's royal family, Archduke Franz Ferdinand, was assassinated by a Serb, Austria-Hungary used the event as an excuse to declare war on Serbia on July 28. The system of alliances then kicked in; one by one, members of the rival alliances declared war on each other.

← Count Alfred von Schlieffen planned Germany's strategy of attacking France.

Timeline
1914
August

August

August 1 Germany Germany declares war on Russia.

August 4 Britain Britain declares war on Germany.

August 7 France The first troops of Britain's 100,000-strong Expeditionary Force arrive in France.

August 3 Germany Germany declares war on Russia's ally, France.

August 4 United States The United States declares itself neutral.

August 5 Belgium Germans fail to take Liege, a key border defense and railroad center.

KEY:

Western Front

Eastern Front

Other fronts

Germany's Motives

Germany was eager to capture valuable coalfields along either side of the French and Belgian border. More importantly, the Schlieffen Plan called for the full-scale invasion and defeat of France before the German armies traveled east to fight the Russians.

As soon as war was declared, therefore, events became inevitable. A race began to mobilize fighting forces and get them into the field. According to contemporary military theory, even a day's delay could mean the difference between ultimate victory and defeat.

↑ The British government's mobilization order was published in 1914.

Mobilization

Peacetime armies were generally far smaller than those in wartime. To get to full strength, armies had to mobilize their troops. They had to summon reservists (men who had military training) from civilian life, equip them, and get them to the war zone. Because millions of men were involved, the process took time. No one wanted to let their opponents gain an advantage, so once one country started mobilizing, everyone else did.

← Germany gave the light cruiser *Breslau* to its Turkish allies as a gift.

August 14 France
First clash of Battle of the Frontiers between France and Germany.

August 23 Belgium
The British Expeditionary Force (BEF) drives back the Germans in another clash of the Battle of the Frontiers.

August 28 North Sea
The British gain the upper hand over the German navy in the Battle of Heligoland Bight.

August 12 Serbia
Austro-Hungarian troops forced to withdraw after five days of fighting.

August 16 Belgium
Liege falls to the Germans.

August 26 East Prussia
The Germans defeat the Russian Second Army at Tannenberg to end the Russian invasion of East Prussia.

The Outbreak of War

The Western Front was the war's major military theater.
The most important parts of the French and German
armies fought from the North Sea to Switzerland.

A German howitzer could lob a large shell accurately up to 10,000 yards (9,140 m). ⟫

Timeline
1914 September–October

September

KEY:

- Western Front
- Eastern Front
- Other fronts

September 5 France
French and British counterattack in the Battle of the Marne.

September 9 France
The Germans suffer their first defeat as they withdraw from near Paris in the Battle of the Marne.

September 9 East Prussia German victory in the Battle of the Masurian Lakes sees heavy Russian losses.

September 15–18 France The Battle of the Aisne. The British and French try to outmaneuver the Germans with little success in the Race to the Sea.

Timeline

August 3, 1914 Germany invades Belgium.

August 4, 1914 Germany rejects Britain's demand that its troops leave Belgium. The British declare war on Germany at 11:00 P.M.

August 4, 1914 The United States declares itself neutral.

August 16, 1914 After days of German shelling, the Belgian port of Liège surrenders.

August 20, 1914 The Germans capture Belgian capital, Brussels.

August 23, 1914 At Mons, the British push back a German attack but then retreat; the clash marks the end of the Battle of the Frontiers.

August 30, 1914 Paris is bombed by the Germans.

≪ The German generals believed they could conquer France in a matter of weeks in 1914.

When war broke out in 1914, France saw a chance to get revenge for its defeat by the Germans in the Franco-Prussian War (1870–1871) and to recover territory it had subsequently lost to Germany on its eastern border. France had called up about 1.3 million troops in five armies. Its strategy was for three armies to launch all-out attacks in order to recapture the lost territory.

France's commander in chief, General Joseph Joffre, realized that the Germans might try to outflank his forces by invading France from farther north, through Belgium. He held back his other two armies to guard against that possibility. While Joffre's suspicion was

(continued, page 12)

October 18–28 France/Belgium The Germans fail to capture key Channel ports; the BEF clashes with the Germans at the First Battle of Ypres.

October 29 Turkey The Turks declare war on the side of the Central powers and shell Russian ports on the Black Sea.

October

October 23 Mesopotamia British forces land in southern Mesopotamia and evict Turkish forces there.

October 29–November 24 Belgium The French and British stop the German advance at Ypres. Both sides start digging in, creating long lines of trenches.

Timeline (continued)

September 5, 1914 The Battle of the Marne sees French and British forces counterattack along the Marne River between Paris and Verdun.

September 9, 1914 After a decisive defeat, the Germans withdraw from near Paris, marking the end of the Battle of the Marne.

September 15–18, 1914 In the Battle of the Aisne, both sides try to outflank each other as part of the Race to the Sea.

October 29–November 24, 1914 The First Battle of Ypres. Germans fail to break through the Allied front; both sides dig trenches that will stretch from the North Sea to the Swiss border.

December 25, 1914 The Christmas truce: German and British soldiers meet in "no-man's land."

British infantry take cover by a French roadside during the Race to the Sea.

correct, he underestimated the size of the potential German attack through Belgium.

Rapid German Gains

The Germans advanced into Belgium, ignoring Belgium's request to remain neutral. As Britain had guaranteed Belgian independence, it now found itself with no option but to declare war on Germany.

The Germans swept through Belgium and forced Allied forces to retreat south into France. By the start of September, the Allies had retreated almost as far as Paris, but a gap had opened in the German front. Backed by new reserve forces, the French and British targeted this weak gap at the Battle of the Marne. The Allied victory forced the Germans to retreat. Germany's

Timeline
1914 November–December

November

November 5–30 Serbia Austro-Hungarian troops launch an advance toward Belgrade, which falls on December 2.

KEY:

 Western Front

 Eastern Front

 Other fronts

November 1 Pacific A German naval squadron badly damages a British squadron off Coronel, in Chile.

November 11–25 Eastern Front After coming close to defeat by the German Ninth Army at Lódz, Russian forces counterattack and drive the enemy back.

gamble on the Schlieffen Plan had failed. There would be no quick victory over France.

Race to the Sea

The two sets of armies were now in eastern France, north of Paris. From late September until November, each side tried to outflank the other to the north in the so-called Race to the Sea. A series of vicious but indecisive battles brought the armies closer to the English Channel, ending in the southern Belgium city of Ypres. Neither side was able to find an open flank to attack the enemy.

Digging In

Both armies were exhausted and short of supplies. As generals retired to their headquarters to plan for the spring of 1915, the soldiers were left to defend their front lines through the winter. They began to dig trenches that soon spread along the length of the Western Front.

British and German troops meet during an unauthorized truce on ⇓ Christmas Day 1914.

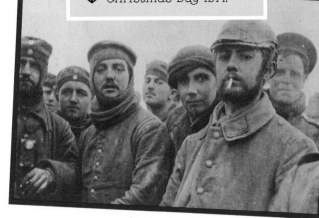

Christmas 1914

On Christmas Day 1914, at a number of places on the Western Front, the bitter enemies of the previous summer and fall climbed out of their trenches under flags of truce. In "no-man's land," they chatted and exchanged gifts of tobacco, alcohol, and chocolate. The military authorities feared that such "fraternization" might make men less willing to fight. They made sure that the truce was not repeated on other Christmas Days during the conflict.

December 8 South Atlantic Ocean
British warships surprise German ships off Argentina, sinking four, including the *Scharnhorst* and the *Gneisenau*.

December 18 Britain The British declare a protectorate over Egypt and move troops to protect the strategically important Suez Canal.

December

December 14 France/Belgium British and French offensives along the Western Front end in stalemate. The First Battle of Champagne continues through the winter.

The Eastern Front

The war on the Eastern Front began badly for Germany and Austria-Hungary, but the two powers recovered quickly and began to launch new attacks.

Some of the 90,000 Russian prisoners captured during the Battle of Tannenberg wait in line for rations. ⟫

Timeline
1915 January–March

January 13 Britain Naval attack on the Dardanelles channel in Turkey is planned.

January 24 North Sea British warships successfully attack German ships in the Battle of the Dogger Bank.

January

February

KEY:

Western Front

Eastern Front

Other fronts

January 19–20 Britain German Zeppelin airships bomb eastern England.

February 1 Germany The government agrees to permit its submarines to sink any ships, even neutral vessels, without warning.

Facing Serbia to the south and Russia to the east, Austria-Hungary's chief of staff, General Franz Conrad von Hötzendorf, could not decide which front should have priority. The result was defeat in both sectors in 1914. The outnumbered Serbs fought the Austro-Hungarians to a standstill in August and September 1914, while the Russians were overrunning much of the Austro-Hungarian province of Galicia.

German Victories

Farther north, where the fighting was between the Germans and Russians, it was a different story. In an attempt to help their ally France, the Russians attacked the German province of East Prussia in August but were defeated at the Battle of Tannenberg. The Russians were not discouraged and tried to restart their offensive. This time, they aimed to strike farther south, from Russia's Polish

Timeline

August 17, 1914 German troops defeat Russian invaders at Stallupönen, East Prussia.

August 24, 1914 German troops delay the Russian advance in East Prussia at the Battle of Orlau-Frankenau. They know the enemy's plans and gather at Tannenberg.

August 26, 1914 Germans attack the Russian Second Army at Tannenberg from the north and south and in the center.

August 29, 1914 By nightfall, the Russians are surrounded. Huge losses include 90,000 prisoners.

(continued page 16)

← In 1914, the war on the Eastern Front was much more open than that on the Western Front.

February 7 East Prussia
Germans successfully attack Russian troops at the Second Battle of the Masurian Lakes.

March 1 Britain
The British begin a naval blockade of Germany.

March

March 10 France The BEF launch an offensive at Neuve-Chapelle, using artillery fire to bombard enemy positions.

March 18 Mediterranean
British and French vessels fail to force a way through the Dardanelles by naval power alone.

Timeline (continued)

September 3, 1914 Russian Fifth Army splits two Austro-Hungarian armies at the Battle of Rava Ruska. By September 11, the Austro-Hungarians have lost 350,000 men.

September 7, 1914 Austro-Hungarian troops launch a second invasion of Serbia at the Battle of the Drina River.

September 9, 1914 Germans score major success as they surround Russian troops at the Masurian Lakes.

November 5–30, 1914 Renewed Austro-Hungarian attacks toward Belgrade see Serbian troops withdraw. Austro-Hungarian troops occupy the Serbian capital on December 2.

December 3–9, 1914 Serbian troops defeat the Austro-Hungarians at the Battle of Kolubra using extra ammunition sent by the French.

territories into the German area of Silesia. The Russian attack was halted by a German advance around Lódz in November. Many of the German troops had arrived by railroad from the Western Front.

The Great Retreat

The Russians defeated Austria-Hungary in the first part of 1915, and the Austro-Hungarian fortress of Przemysl surrendered. General Erich von Falkenhayn, the new German chief of the general staff, planned to focus on the Western Front, but Emperor Wilhelm II ordered him to give the Eastern Front priority. Von Falkenhayn sent troops east.

The German and Austro-Hungarian armies began their offensive around the towns of Gorlice and Tarnow in Galicia in May 1915. By the start of June, the Germans had broken through. The Russians began what they called the "great retreat," which did not stop until the bad weather of the fall. By then, the

Cooks prepare food for German troops in the field during the defense of East Prussia. ⇓

Timeline
1915
April–
June

April 5 France A French attack in Meuse-Argonne makes little progress.

April 22 Belgium Second Battle of Ypres. The Germans use poisonous gas for the first time, causing panic among British troops.

May 7 Atlantic Ocean A German submarine sinks the passenger liner *Lusitania*, killing many US citizens.

April

May

KEY:

Western Front

Eastern Front

Other fronts

April 8 Turkey Turks begin a massacre in which one million Armenians will die.

April 25 Turkey Allied landings on the Gallipoli Peninsula fail to achieve their initial objectives.

April 26 Italy Italy joins the war against its former ally, Austria-Hungary.

↑ Captured Russian soldiers in Lódz await transportation to take them to prison camps.

Germans had advanced more than 300 miles (480 km). Czar Nicholas II, the Russian ruler, fired his top commander and took command of his forces himself.

Heavy Losses

The fighting in 1915 cost the Russians about one million men killed and wounded, and another million taken prisoner. The Central powers' successes also came at a price. Together, Germany and Austria-Hungary had about one million casualties on the Eastern Front. Late in 1915, Bulgaria joined on the Central powers' side and helped end the stubborn Serbian resistance.

Battle of Tannenberg

On August 24, 1914, German troops successfully delayed the advance of Russian troops by a day in East Prussia. This gave the Germans time to concentrate at Tannenberg. The Russians did not realize that the Germans were listening to their radio messages and knew their plans. By August 29, the Germans had the Russian army surrounded. Tannenberg was a major German victory. Russian losses were huge.

May 9 France The British suffer heavy casualties at Neuve-Chapelle. The French open the Second Battle of Artois.

May 26 Britain Naval chief Sir Winston Churchill is fired after the failure of his planned naval attack at Gallipoli.

June

May 19 Turkey Outnumbered Australians and New Zealanders defeat a Turkish attack at Gallipoli.

May 24 Belgium There are heavy losses on both sides in the Second Battle of Ypres.

June 23–July Italy First Battle of the Isonzo between Italians and Austro-Hungarians sees heavy casualties and little progress.

Failure at Gallipoli

The Ottoman Turks controlled the Dardanelles, which linked the Mediterranean with the Black Sea. The Allies had to seize the strait to get equipment to the Russians.

A shell explodes near a pier used by the British to land troops and supplies at Gallipoli. →

Timeline
1915
July–September

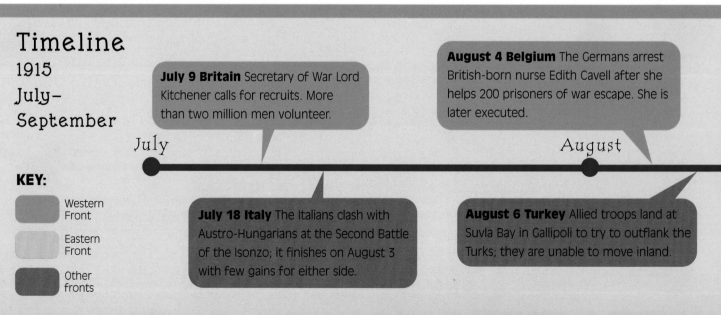

July 9 Britain Secretary of War Lord Kitchener calls for recruits. More than two million men volunteer.

August 4 Belgium The Germans arrest British-born nurse Edith Cavell after she helps 200 prisoners of war escape. She is later executed.

July

August

KEY:

Western Front

Eastern Front

Other fronts

July 18 Italy The Italians clash with Austro-Hungarians at the Second Battle of the Isonzo; it finishes on August 3 with few gains for either side.

August 6 Turkey Allied troops land at Suvla Bay in Gallipoli to try to outflank the Turks; they are unable to move inland.

At the start of 1915, Britain's navy minister, Winston Churchill, convinced other Allied leaders to attack Turkey. He aimed to reopen the supply route to Russia through the Black Sea and to knock Germany's weakest partner out of the war. An Allied fleet bombarded Turkish forts on either side of the Dardanelles in February.

Naval Attack

A full-scale naval attack destroyed many of the Turkish coastal guns. Unknown to the Allies, however, the guns that were not damaged were low on ammunition. A sustained attack might have allowed Allied ships to sail to Constantinople (now Istanbul) and force the Turks to surrender. However, four Allied battleships struck mines and sank. The naval attack was called off.

Gallipoli

The Allies now decided to invade the Gallipoli Peninsula on the north side of the

Poor planning led to the Allies' defeat on the Gallipoli campaign.

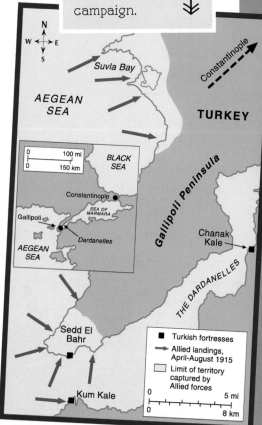

Timeline

March 18, 1915 Final Anglo-French attempt fails to force a way through the Dardanelles by naval power alone.

April 25, 1915 Anglo-French invasion of the Gallipoli Peninsula begins badly. The Turks occupy the hilltops, from where they can fire down on the Allied troops landing on the beaches.

May 6, 1915 The British at Gallipoli fail to capture the town of Krithia and lose 6,500 men in the process.

May 19, 1915 Australians and New Zealanders at Gallipoli—17,000 men—defeat 40,000 Turkish soldiers, inflicting more than 3,000 casualties.

June 4, 1915 30,000 British troops again fail to capture Krithia.

(continued page 20)

August 12 Britain Work starts on first tracked armored vehicle, or "tank."

September

September 27–28 Mesopotamia The British successfully attack Turks at Kut-el-Amara on the Tigris River.

September 18 Russia The Germans capture Vilna; in only a few months, they have forced the Russians to retreat 300 miles (480 km), out of Galicia and Poland.

September 25 France French attacks start Second Battle of Champagne and Battle of Artois. British attack in Battle of Loos.

Timeline (continued)

December 8, 1915
Evacuation of Allied positions begins at Suvla Bay and Ari Burna at Gallipoli. The Turks do not interfere. Some 83,000 men, 186 artillery pieces, and 1,700 vehicles, together with some 4,500 transport animals, are taken off the Gallipoli Peninsula by boat.

January 8, 1916 The Allied evacuation of the Gallipoli Peninsula is completed. The campaign has cost 252,000 British, Commonwealth, and French men and the Turks around 250,000 men.

⌅   After months of unsuccessful attacks and increasing casualties, the British leave Gallipoli.

Dardanelles and advance on land toward the Turkish capital. However, it took weeks to get an invasion force ready. The Turks used the time to move defenders to the area. When the Allies began landing on April 25, the Turks had enough troops on the hills inland to hold them on the beaches. The Turkish commanders were helped by poor leadership and organization on the Allied side.

The Allied troops, many of whom were from the Australia and New Zealand Army Corps (ANZAC), soon found what had been planned as a great strategic maneuver turned into a version of the Western Front. There were few

Australian troops advance with fixed bayonets against the Turkish trenches at Gallipoli. ⇒

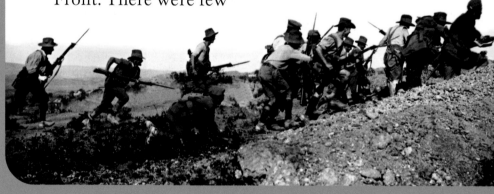

Timeline
1915
October–
December

October 6 Serbia German and Austro-Hungarian armies invade Serbia from the north; two Bulgarian armies invade from the east. The Serbian army retreats southwest.

October   November

KEY:

 Western Front

 Eastern Front

 Other fronts

October 6 France The French launch a new offensive in the Second Battle of Champagne, but it runs out of steam with few gains.

October 13–14 France The Battle of Loos ends with small British gains; there is increasing criticism of the commander of the BEF, Sir John French.

alternatives to frontal attacks on tough enemy positions on hills overlooking the Allied trenches.

The Landings Abandoned

The Allies tried to restart their advance by making landings on an additional beachhead in August. The Turks were surprised, but poor British leadership again destroyed the slim chances of success.

A new British commander took over in October and recommended the landing force be evacuated. Pulling out was dangerous, but the operation was well planned and carried out. No Allied lives were lost during the two-stage withdrawal in December 1915 and January 1916. However, in the earlier fighting each side had suffered about 250,000 casualties.

Mustafa Kemal

The Turkish resistance to the initial Anglo-French landings at Gallipoli was commanded by Mustafa Kemal. His energy and drive were key to avoiding Turkish defeat. Kemal became a hero to many Turks. After Turkey's defeat, he became head of an alternative Turkish government and led a march on the capital, Ankara, to drive out occupying forces. Kemal became president of the new Republic of Turkey in 1923. In 1934, he was given the name Ataturk, "Father of Turks."

November 10–December 2 Italy
Italians and Austro-Hungarians fight the Fourth Battle of the Isonzo.

December 17 Britain
General Sir Douglas Haig becomes commander of the British Expeditionary Force.

December

November 22–26 Mesopotamia
British forces attack Turkish positions at Ctesiphon but are forced to retreat to Kut-al-Amara.

December 3 France General Joseph Joffre becomes commander in chief of all French forces on the Western Front.

December 8 Turkey
Turks allow Allied evacuation to begin at Gallipoli.

The War at Sea

The war at sea between Britain and Germany was played out across the North Atlantic Ocean, where the Germans used U-boats (submarines) for the first time.

German warships of the ➤➤
High Seas Fleet sail into
the North Sea to confront
the British at Jutland.

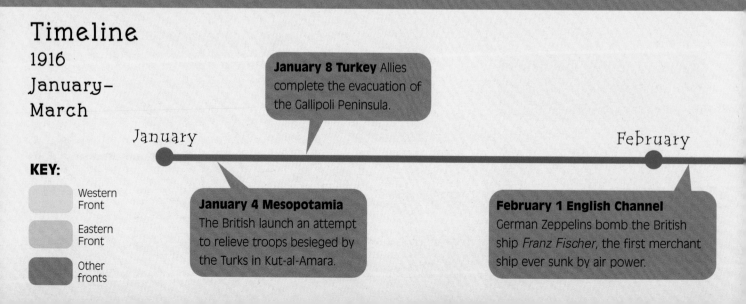

Timeline
1916
January–
March

January   February

KEY:

> **January 8 Turkey** Allies complete the evacuation of the Gallipoli Peninsula.

Western
Front

Eastern
Front

Other
fronts

January 4 Mesopotamia
The British launch an attempt to relieve troops besieged by the Turks in Kut-al-Amara.

February 1 English Channel
German Zeppelins bomb the British ship *Franz Fischer*, the first merchant ship ever sunk by air power.

At the start of the war in 1914, Britain had the world's strongest navy and its largest merchant fleet. However, Germany had begun to build a strong navy of its own to threaten Britain's position. When the conflict began, Britain imposed a naval blockade. Within days of the war's start, almost all of Germany's merchant ships had been captured or had taken refuge in neutral ports.

Besides its larger fleet, Britain's geographical position blocked German access to the oceans. To reach the high seas, Germany had to defeat the Royal Navy. For Britain, meanwhile, defeat would mean that the war was lost. The responsibility for victory lay with the Grand Fleet's commander, Admiral John Jellicoe.

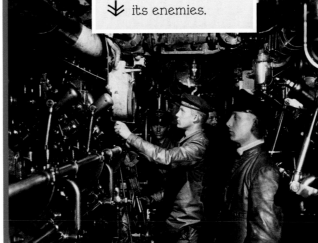

Germany's U-boats (engine room below) were key to stopping supplies reaching ↓ its enemies.

The Battle of Jutland

Only one large battle, the Battle of Jutland (the Battle of Skagerrak for the Germans), was fought between the two fleets on May 31, 1916, in the North Sea, 50 miles

Timeline

August 28, 1914 British and German vessels clash in the Battle of Heligoland Bight in the North Sea; the Germans lose four vessels.

September 22, 1914 The German submarine U-9 sinks three British cruisers with the loss of 1,400 men.

November 3, 1914 German warships in the North Sea bombard Britain's east coast. Raids reach a peak on December 16, when the ports of Whitby and Hartlepool are attacked, causing more than 700 casualties.

December 8, 1914 The British sink four out of five German warships in a surprise attack at the Battle of the Falkland Islands, in the south Atlantic off Argentina.

(continued page 24)

February 21 France Germans attack the strategically vital fortified town of Verdun.

February 25 France The Germans take key French position at Verdun; General Henri-Philippe Pétain takes charge of French troops.

March 18 Russia Russians suffer heavy losses for little gain in the First Battle of Lake Naroch.

March

February 22 France The French create a key supply road to Verdun, "the Sacred Way."

March 11 Italy The Fifth Battle of the Isonzo starts.

Timeline (continued)

January 24, 1915
The Battle of the Dogger Bank sees a victory for Britain's faster and better-armed warships.

May 7, 1915 The liner *Lusitania* is sunk by the German submarine U-20; among the dead are 128 US citizens.

May 31, 1916 In the Battle of Jutland (Skagerrak), the Germans sink three British battleships, three cruisers, and eight destroyers; the Germans lose one battleship, four cruisers, and five destroyers. Ultimately, however, the battle is a British victory that restricts the German High Fleet to its home ports.

March 18, 1917 Three US vessels are sunk by German submarines. The incident further angers the United States.

A German submarine ⌖ crew watches an Italian merchant ship burn.

(80 km) off the coast of Denmark. Despite having the upper hand early in the clash, the Germans later retreated as the British gained control.

After Jutland, the British blockade remained as effective as ever. The German fleet remained in port for the rest of the war, contributing nothing to the war effort.

Submarine Warfare

World War I was the first conflict in which submarines were used. Germany's U-boats (*unterseeboots*) were a new technology, and their development before 1914 had been very slow. In February 1915, Germany began to use them for its own blockade, sinking merchant ships carrying cargo to and from Britain. This period of submarine attacks lasted until September 1915.

The Strategy Fails

The Germans renewed their attacks briefly in 1916, but stopped them after US protests. However, they then decided that the danger of drawing the United States

Timeline
1916
April–June

KEY:

- Western Front
- Eastern Front
- Other fronts

April

May

April 9 France The Germans capture French front-line trenches on "Dead Man" Ridge at Verdun.

April 29 Mesopotamia The besieged British surrender to the Turks at Kut-al-Amara.

April 21 Ireland The Easter Rising. Irish nationalists, mainly in Dublin, launch a failed revolt against British rule.

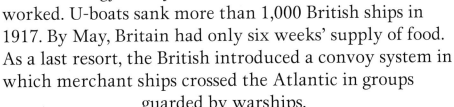

The British liner *Lusitania* was sunk by a German submarine. →

into the war was a risk they had to take and resumed the attacks.

The strategy nearly worked. U-boats sank more than 1,000 British ships in 1917. By May, Britain had only six weeks' supply of food. As a last resort, the British introduced a convoy system in which merchant ships crossed the Atlantic in groups guarded by warships.

The tactic worked. British shipping losses in 1918 were less than half of those in 1917. The U-boat campaign had failed to starve Britain into defeat. Instead, it proved to be the main reason the United States joined the war in April 1917.

← Britain's HMS *Dreadnought* marked a new era in warship design.

The Sinking of the Lusitania

On May 7, 1915, the German submarine U-20 attacked the British passenger liner *Lusitania* as it sailed off the west coast of Ireland. In just 18 minutes, the ship sank, killing 1,198 people, including 128 Americans. A luxury liner, the *Lusitania* had sailed across the Atlantic without incident during the first months of the war. Its sinking caused outrage, especially in the United States, because it had come without warning. The incident led to the United States declaring war on Germany.

May 13 Arabia Arabs capture the Islamic holy city of Mecca from the Turks.

May 27 United States President Woodrow Wilson suggests the creation of an international body to maintain peace; the body will become the League of Nations.

June 7 France After bitter fighting, the Germans capture Fort Vaux at Verdun.

June

May 31 North Sea Both British and German fleets suffer losses at the Battle of Jutland.

June 4 Russia Russians launch attack against Austro-Hungarians and Germans to concide with a planned British attack on the Somme River in France.

June 17 Italy Austro-Hungarians stop their Trentino Offensive as casualties mount.

The Struggle at Verdun

By 1916, it was clear there were no quick victories to be won on the Western Front. The Germans chose to attack the fortified town of Verdun, on the border with France.

The painting *The Ravine of the Dead* captures the horrors of the fighting around Verdun in 1916. →

Timeline
1916
July–September

KEY:

- Western Front
- Eastern Front
- Other fronts

July 4 Germany German naval chiefs recommend using submarines against British merchant ships.

August 4 Italy The Sixth Battle of the Isonzo starts.

July

August

July 1 France British Somme Offensive starts. British casualties of 60,000 are greatest loss ever in a single day's combat.

July 10 Russia Russians have captured 300,000 prisoners since Brusilov Offensive started.

Verdun, about 120 miles (192 km) east of Paris, was a major strongpoint on the French border. German chief of staff Erich von Falkenhayn guessed correctly that the French would commit everything to hold it.

A Slogging Match

The attack began on February 21, 1916. After four days, the Germans captured Fort Douaumont. They believed they had won a great victory.

In fact, the French high command had decided to hold Verdun despite the loss of the fort. Reinforcements were arriving, and a new commander, General Henri-Philippe Pétain, reorganized the French, who began to use their artillery more effectively. The battlefield turned into a scene of slaughter on both sides, but gradually the German front line crept forward. Pétain was promoted, and Robert Nivelle took his place.

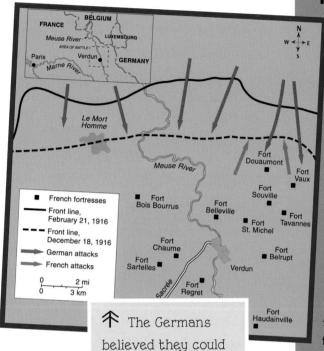

↑ The Germans believed they could win at Verdun, but the battle ended in a stalemate.

Timeline

February 21, 1916 The German offensive begins. The main attack is by 140,000 men of Crown Prince William's Fifth Army. The French are pushed back.

February 22, 1916 The French create La Voie Sacrée ("The Sacred Way"). This narrow road to Verdun becomes the main route for supplies and reinforcements entering the city. Around Verdun, German attacks gain some ground but are met by fierce French counterattacks.

February 25, 1916 One of the key French positions at Verdun, Fort Douaumont, falls to Germans. General Pétain takes charge of French troops.

June 7, 1916 After weeks of bitter fighting, the Germans capture Fort Vaux from the French.

(continued page 28)

September 17 France German air ace Baron Manfred von Richthofen scores his first victory.

September

August 29 Germany Field Marshal Paul von Hindenburg becomes chief of the general staff; General Erich Ludendorff becomes his deputy.

September 15 France Using tanks for the first time on the Western Front, the British break the deadlock on the Somme by capturing the villages of Flers and Courcelette.

Timeline (continued)

June 22, 1916 The Germans attack again, using a new type of poison gas that the French gas masks do not protect against.

October 24, 1916 The French attack northeast of Verdun. They retake Fort Douaumont, with 6,000 prisoners.

December 15, 1916 The French attack to the northeast of Verdun. Within a few days, they force the Germans away from key positions, including Forts Douaumont and Vaux. The attack ends the main Battle of Verdun. Losses are huge: 360,000 French troops and 336,000 German troops. The German plan to destroy the French army has failed.

Le Mort Homme Ridge ⟶ ("Dead Man" Ridge) at Verdun shows the results of prolonged artillery fire.

Attack After Attack

By early June 1916, the Germans were pushing forward again. Verdun seemed certain to fall. Pétain—or possibly Nivelle—issued special orders, which included France's most famous slogan of the war: "Ils ne passeront pas!" ("They shall not pass!"). Somehow, the French held on.

On July 1, the British began their attack on the Somme River sector. Soon the Germans had to withdraw troops from Verdun in order to reinforce their defenses there. Attacks and counterattacks at Verdun continued until Field Marshal Paul von Hindenburg and General Erich Ludendorff, who took over the German army in August, halted all German attacks at Verdun. Both realized that the plan to destroy the French army had little chance of success.

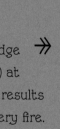

Timeline
1916
October–
December

October

KEY:

- Western Front
- Eastern Front
- Other fronts

October 16 Arabia British Captain T. E. Lawrence ("Lawrence of Arabia") becomes an adviser to Prince Feisal, who is leading an Arab revolt against the Turks.

November

October 7 United States Woodrow Wilson is reelected as president.

October 10 Russia Czar Nicholas orders the end of the successful Brusilov Offensive.

French backup travels to Verdun along "the Sacred Way," a vital supply line.

Now the French launched a counterattack. They recaptured Fort Douaumont on October 24 and regained much of the ground they had lost. Their attacks continued until the battle was finally halted on December 18. In the last three days of fighting, the French captured nearly 120,000 Germans.

About one million men had been killed or wounded, just over half on the French side. Yet little had been achieved. Both sides were virtually back where they had started by the close of the fighting. Erich von Falkenhayn had hoped to smash the French army, but both armies had suffered equally. Neither side could claim victory.

General Henri-Philippe Pétain

After the start of war, Pétain was so good at his job that he quickly rose through the ranks until he took command at Verdun in 1916. Pétain made sure that his soldiers had food and medical care. That ended their frequent mutinies and ensured the French could fight into 1918. However, after World War II, Pétain was tried as a traitor for cooperating with the Nazis.

General Pétain was one of France's greatest heroes.

December 5 Britain Prime Minister Herbert Asquith resigns and is replaced by David Lloyd George.

December 13 Mesopotamia A British offensive begins along the Tigris River; progress is slow.

December

December 6 Romania The Germans enter Bucharest.

December 15 France The Battle of Verdun ends. Losses on both sides have been huge.

Slaughter on the Somme

British forces, helped by troops from Commonwealth countries, took the leading Allied role in the bloody Battle of the Somme in 1916. Many lost their lives.

British troops rest near a Mark I tank during a lull in the fighting on the Somme. ⇉

Timeline
1917
January–March

January 19 Mexico British decode the Zimmerman telegram, a secret German suggestion of an alliance with Mexico if the United States declares war on Germany.

January 31 Germany The Germans launch unrestricted submarine warfare.

January

February

February 3 United States The United States cuts diplomatic ties with Germany over unrestricted submarine warfare.

KEY:

 Western Front

 Eastern Front

 Other fronts

The British role in the Somme Offensive was increased because French troops were preoccupied by the struggle at Verdun. The Somme River region was chosen because it was where the two Allied armies met, not because it was a good place to attack. The Germans held strong defensive positions on high ground overlooking the Allied lines.

Using Artillery

Key to the plans of British general Douglas Haig was a huge amount of artillery and shells. The British believed that they had assembled enough supplies at the Somme for a decisive barrage. They were wrong. More than one quarter of the shells did not explode, and those that did were poor at blasting gaps in barbed wire and useless for smashing defensive positions, the two prime purposes of the artillery bombardment.

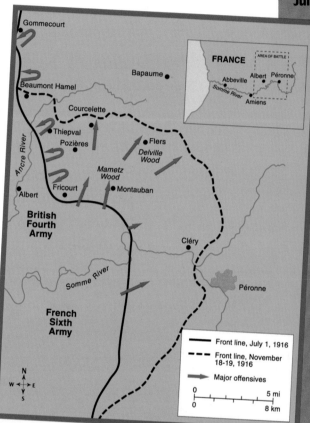

Timeline

June 24, 1916 The British begin shelling German trenches around the Somme River. Some 1.7 million shells are fired on the first day, but they fail to damage German barbed wire or their strongly constructed defenses.

July 1, 1916 The Somme Offensive begins. The attacking British infantry are confronted by uncut German barbed wire and intact defenses and meet a wall of machine-gun fire. Casualties are the greatest ever suffered by the British in a single day's fighting.

July 14, 1916 A British advance almost breaks through German lines, but reserves arrive too late.

(continued page 32)

⇐ At the Somme, the British advanced only 6 miles (10 km) and suffered 400,000 casualties.

February 23 France
Germans withdraw to newly built Hindenburg Line, 20 miles (32 km) behind existing line.

March 12 Russia Revolutionaries and the Russian parliament establish rival governments.

March 18 Atlantic Ocean German submarines sink three US vessels.

March

March 8 Russia Demonstrations and riots in Moscow against food and fuel shortages; based on the Russian calendar, the event is called the "February Revolution."

March 15 Russia Czar Nicholas II abdicates.

March 26 Palestine First Battle of Gaza sees British invasion of Turkish Palestine fail.

Timeline (continued)

August 1, 1916 The Somme Offensive is a month old: British casualties total 158,000; German losses are 160,000.

September 15, 1916 The British begin an offensive to break the deadlock; tanks appear on the Western Front for the first time. The British capture two villages, Flers and Courcelette, but the slow-moving tanks are not a success, although they initially panic German troops.

November 18, 1916 The Battle of the Ancre marks the end of the British offensive on the Somme. At the end of their attacks, the British have still not captured some of their initial objectives.

↑ A British mine explodes underneath the German trenches near Beaumont Hamel.

Disaster on Day One

Following the artillery bombardment, the British infantry climbed out of their trenches to advance. But the German front lines remained intact. The British were mowed down, many before they had gone more than a few yards. Some of them got across no-man's land, only to find the German barbed wire still in place. As they tried to find a way through, many more men were machine-gunned down. Almost 20,000 British soldiers died on July 1, 1916, and another 40,000 were wounded. It was a disastrous day for the British army, the worst in its history.

In the weeks that followed, there were many chances for both sides to get the upper hand, but they were

British troops advance toward German lines in the Battle of the Somme. ⟫

Timeline
1917 April–June

April 3 Russia Russian revolutionary Lenin returns from exile and starts his plans to take control of the country.

April 9 France British make good gains in the Battle of Arras.

April 17 France French troops mutiny.

April ●————————————————————————————————● May

April 6 United States The United States declares war on Germany.

April 16–20 France General Robert Nivelle launches a major French offensive in Champagne and along the Aisne River; having captured plans for the attack, the Germans defeat the advance easily.

KEY:
- Western Front
- Eastern Front
- Other fronts

missed. There were no portable radios to quickly pass messages, and so it took hours to carry out orders or maneuvers, giving the enemy time to rebuild their positions. Despite some small gains on both sides, the front lines remained largely stationary.

Ending the Battle

On September 15, 1916, the British used their new secret weapon, the tank, for the first time ever in the Battle of Flers-Courcelette. The tanks were clumsy and unreliable. The British captured some ground, but by the end of the day, hardly any of the tanks were working.

By the end of the battle, the British had advanced no more than 6 miles (10 km) from their starting positions. Some 125,000 British Empire troops had died in the process, along with 50,000 Frenchmen. No one knows how many Germans died: estimates range from about 100,000 to 160,000. For every man killed on each side, roughly three more were wounded. Neither side achieved a clear victory in the Battle of the Somme.

Haig led British → forces on the Western Front.

Field Marshal Sir Douglas Haig

Douglas Haig was the commander in chief of the British troops on the Western Front from December 1915 to the end of the war. After planning and leading the major British offensives at the Somme in 1916, he was promoted to field marshal, despite the attack's failure. Haig was a skilled organizer who worked well with his French allies. But Haig was criticized for the high number of casualties he lost in battle.

May 9 France General Nivelle's offensive fails.

June 7 Belgium British forces capture the Messines Ridge, which allows the big offensive of Passchendaele, or Third Battle of Ypres.

June

May 10 Britain Lloyd George orders British Royal Navy to accompany merchant ships in convoy to protect them. Merchant ship sinkings fall.

May 23 Britain German bombers attack London from Belgian bases.

A Pivotal Year

Both sides began 1917 with new plans for the Western Front. The French and British both planned major offensives for the spring to crush the Germans.

Canadian troops start to dig in after their victory on Vimy Ridge. →

Timeline
1917
July–September

July 24 France The Dutch dancer Mata Hari stands trial as a German spy; she is later found guilty and executed.

July 31 Belgium Third Battle of Ypres begins.

August 2 Russia General Lavr Kornilov replaces Aleksey Brusilov as Russia's commander in chief.

July

August

July 18 Belgium The British begin a preliminary bombardment before their attack in the Ypres region.

August 2 Belgium The British offensive at Ypres is temporarily halted after heavy rain turns the ground to mud; the offensive resumes on August 16, when the ground is drier.

KEY:

Western Front

Eastern Front

Other fronts

↑ Woodrow Wilson requests the US Congress to support war with Germany.

After the terrible casualties the German army suffered in 1916, General Erich Ludendorff decided on a new strategy for 1917. He ordered the German army to stop counterattacking every Allied advance. He also withdrew his troops from a large area of captured French territory to a strong new defensive system, the Hindenburg Line, from which he would attack the Allied forces. The German retreat forced the French to change their plans.

Timeline

April 9, 1917 The British begin the Battle of Arras to try to force the Germans to withdraw from the Aisne River sector, which the French are about to attack; they make gains on the first day but lose many aircraft shot down by the Germans.

April 11, 1917 The Battle of Arras becomes a stalemate as German resistance grows; by the time it ends in mid-May, British casualties are 150,000, German casualties are 100,000.

April 16–20, 1917 General Nivelle's French offensive along the Aisne River fails because Germans know his plans in advance.

April 17, 1917 Nivelle's troops mutiny and abandon their posts.

May 9, 1917 Nivelle's offensive fails; the French have suffered huge losses: 187,000 men versus German losses of 163,000.

(continued page 36)

September 20 Belgium The focus of the British offensives at Ypres switches to the south of the region.

September

September 1 Russia German stormtroopers capture the town of Riga; many Russian soldiers simply desert their posts.

September 27–28 Mesopotamia After defeating the Turks at the Battle of Ramadi, the British pursue them deep into central Mesopotamia.

Timeline (continued)

June 7, 1917 British troops capture Messines Ridge in southwest Belgium, paving the way for the Third Battle of Ypres, or Battle of Passchendaele.

July 31, 1917 The battle begins with British advances of just 2 miles (3 km).

October 12, 1917 The British focus at Ypres switches to the village of Passchendaele.

November 6, 1917 The British finally take Passchendaele; casualties on both sides are high.

November 20, 1917 The Battle of Cambrai is the first major tank-led battle.

The Battle of Passchendaele was the British army's major offensive in 1917. →

The French Mutinies

In April 1917, French commander Robert Nivelle launched a new offensive, the Second Battle of the Aisne, but it rapidly stalled. The French soldiers had had enough. In addition to their losses, they had to put up with awful food, almost no leave, and poor medical services. In April 1917, thousands mutinied. Nivelle was fired and replaced by General Henri-Philippe Pétain, who addressed the soldiers' concerns and ended the mutinies.

Passchendaele

In July 1917, Douglas Haig launched an offensive around the Belgian town of Ypres after a long artillery barrage. Even though the British had more artillery and air superiority, ground conditions and weather favored the defense. Torrential rain fell as artillery shells turned the battlefield

- - - Front line, July 31, 1917
——— Front line, November 10, 1917
→ Major British offensives

0 ___ 4 mi
0 ___ 6 km

NORTH SEA
Zeebrugge
Ostend
Nieuport
BELGIUM
AREA OF BATTLE
Passchendaele
Ypres
Messines
FRANCE

Merckem
German Fifth Army
Bixschoote
Langemarck
Poelcappelle
German Fourth Army
Pilckem
Passchendaele
Boesinghe
British Fifth Army
Broodseinde
Zonnebeke
N W E S
Ypres
British Second Army
Zillebeke
Gheluvelt

Timeline
1917 October– December

October 12 Belgium British offensive at Ypres switches to Passchendaele.

October 26 Belgium A new British offensive begins at Passchendaele.

October

November

October 24 Italy The Austro-Hungarians launch the Twelfth Battle of the Isonzo (Battle of Caporetto), making good advances.

November 6 Belgium The British finally capture Passchendaele.

KEY:
Western Front
Eastern Front
Other fronts

into a swamp. The British attacked until mid-November, switching their target to the village of Passchendaele. In all, they lost about 300,000 casualties for a 5-mile (8 km) advance.

Massed Tank Attack

The Battle of Cambrai in November was the world's first tank-led battle. Some 320 British tanks smashed a gap in the German lines, but over half broke down or were destroyed on the first day. With no reserves, the British were pushed back.

The year ended with the armies on the Western Front having suffered huge casualties with little apparent gain.

↑ An aerial view of the Nivelle Offensive. It was France's only major attack in 1917.

Tanks

The British had developed tanks from farm tractors that were fitted with caterpillar tracks to prevent them sinking into the ground. The new weapons were first used on a large scale at Cambrai in November 1917. Although the tanks were unreliable, they could create gaps in the German lines. The Germans later built their own tanks, but mainly used British tanks recovered from various battlefields.

⇐ British troops attempt to free a light field gun from the mud at Ypres.

November 20 France
The first big tank battle, the Battle of Cambrai, begins.

December 5 France The Battle of Cambrai ends; it suggested that massed tanks could lead a breakout on the Western Front.

December

November 13–15 Palestine
British troops break through Turkish defenses at the Battle of Junction Station.

December 9 Palestine
The British take Jerusalem as the Turks abandon the city.

Germany's Last Gamble

At the start of 1918, Germany was in a bad position.
American troops were on the way to Europe. The
Germans planned one last offensive before they arrived.

British and French
troops man hastily built
defenses at the start of
Operation Michael. ⇒

Timeline
1918
January–
March

January 8 United States President
Wilson outlines his Fourteen Points, a
peace program to end the war.

February 18 Russia Irritated
by Bolshevik delays in peace
negotiations, German forces
move deeper into Russia.

January   February

KEY:

Western
Front

Eastern
Front

Other
fronts

January 27 Mesopotamia With Russia in
turmoil following the revolution, a British force
sets out to take control of Russian oil wells on
the Caspian Sea.

General Erich Ludendorff correctly realized that the Allies' greatest weakness was that they did not always work together. The French priority was to guard Paris, while the British wanted to defend northern France and the English Channel. In March 1918, he planned Operation Michael: an attack on Amiens in France to drive the British north and the French south.

Series of Offensives

To achieve his plan, Ludendorff trained stormtroopers—elite infantry—to advance after the initial bombardment. However, since the stormtroopers got the best rations and weapons, morale in the rest of the German army fell.

↑ Stormtroopers go forward at the opening of Operation Michael.

The German attack began on March 21, 1918. By the end of the first day, the British were in retreat and had lost 20,000 men as prisoners. By March 25, the Germans had advanced about 25 miles (40 km), farther and faster

Timeline

March 21, 1918 Operation Michael begins with German stormtroopers easily overwhelming British troops.

March 23, 1918 The Germans begin bombardment of Paris that will last until August 9.

March 27, 1918 German troops are close to Amiens, but their attack is stopped by Allied troops 10 miles (16 km) to the east.

April 5, 1918 Operation Michael is halted; the Germans have advanced 40 miles (64 km), but both sides have suffered heavy casualties.

April 9–10, 1918 Ludendorff opens Operation Georgette. The Germans win early gains.

(continued page 40)

March 3 Russia Bolsheviks, fighting a civil war, are forced to give up much territory in the Brest-Litovsk peace treaty with the Germans.

March 21 France German general Ludendorff launches Operation Michael, planned as a knockout blow before US troops arrive on the Western Front.

March

March 23 Paris The Germans start bombardment of Paris. It lasts until August 9.

March 29 France US air ace Eddie Rickenbacker scores his first kill; by the end of the war, he will have 26 air victories.

Timeline (continued)

April 17, 1918 British and French troops around Ypres halt a German advance toward the ports of northern France; both sides have lost around 100,000 men.

April 23, 1918 The British launch a surprise amphibious assault on the Belgian ports of Ostend and Zeebrugge to stop German submarines operating in the English Channel, but the raid is a failure.

May 28, 1918 US forces make their first attack of the war around Cantigny, which they capture with the loss of 1,600 men.

June 5, 1918 Ludendorff halts all German attacks.

June 6, 1918 US forces attack at Belleau Wood, which they capture after three weeks of fighting; US losses are 1,800 men killed and 7,000 wounded.

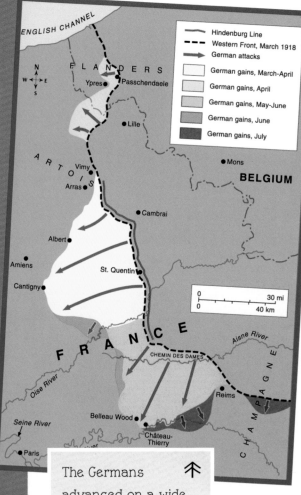

The Germans advanced on a wide front, but were ultimately halted.

than in any other battle since 1914.

The next day, the Allies appointed General Ferdinand Foch to coordinate operations on the Western Front. The Allies began to work together more effectively. Seeing that further efforts to drive them apart were useless, Ludendorff halted the offensive on April 5.

Renewed Attacks

Soon Ludendorff began a new attack, this time around Ypres in Belgium, in the British-held sector of the front. This operation, Georgette, began on April 9; again, desperate Allied defense held it up after it made initial gains.

Ludendorff still believed that the British were his toughest opponents, but he did not want to attack them until he had drawn Allied reserves south. He moved his

Timeline
1918
April–
June

April 5 France General Ludendorff halts Operation Michael.

April 9–10 France/Belgium Ludendorff launches Operation Georgette, an offensive along the Lys River aimed at the ports of the English Channel through which the British receive their supplies.

April

May

April 17 France/Belgium British and French troops halt the Lys River offensive near Ypres.

April 21 Western Front German pilot Baron Manfred von Richthofen is shot down and killed. He was the most successful air ace of the war.

KEY:

Western Front

Eastern Front

Other fronts

artillery and his remaining stormtroopers south to the
Chemin des Dames area of the Aisne River sector,
where he launched an attack on May 27. Helped by
poor defensive tactics, the Germans defeated the Allies
along a 25-mile (40 km) front.

American Arrival

Now, however, the newly arrived US troops played a
key part in the fighting for the first time. At Château-
Thierry, the US Third Division halted a German
advance across the Marne. The US Second Division
suffered heavy casualties but helped drive the Germans
back in the Battle of Belleau Wood, capturing the wood
after three weeks.

Ludendorff knew he had to attack to keep the
advantage. He began
an offensive along
the Marne, but
was soon pushed
back by Allied
counterattacks. On
August 8, thousands
of German troops
began to surrender.
It was now clear
that Germany could
not win the war.

Stormtroopers in World War I

The role of
Germany's elite
stormtroopers was
to penetrate as
deeply and quickly
into enemy territory
as they could. The
first wave made no
attempt to capture
frontline enemy
strongpoints. They
bypassed them for
follow-up troops to
deal with. The
tactic was also
used to great
effect at the
start of World
War II in 1939.

← German
howitzers advance
during Operation
Michael.

May 28 France US forces
undertake their first attack
at Cantigny.

June 4 France Ludendorff calls off
his latest offensive, which has run out
of steam.

June

May 27 France Ludendorff launches a
third offensive of the year, this time on
the Aisne River; the Germans advance
10 miles (16 km) on the first day.

June 6 France US forces
attack at Belleau Wood. It
takes three weeks to
capture the wood.

June 15–22 Italy In the Battle
of the Piave River, the Italians
halt and then turn back an
Austro-Hungarian advance.

US Pressure Counts

Simultaneous Allied offensives drove the Germans back on the Western Front. One of these was the Meuse-Argonne Offensive, the largest US action of the war.

As the Allies advanced, they took large numbers of German prisoners. ⇒

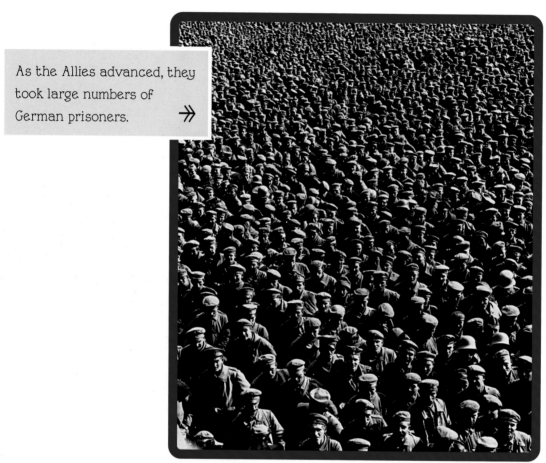

Timeline
1918
July–September

July 16–17 Russia Bolsheviks murder the Russian royal family, including Czar Nicholas II.

August 6 France The Second Battle of the Marne ends disastrously for the Germans.

July

August

KEY:

Western Front

Eastern Front

Other fronts

July 15–17 France French troops are ready for a major German offensive along the Marne River and stop the German advance.

July 18 France The Second Battle of the Marne sees French, British, and U.S. forces attack; German defenses collapse.

The offensive, which began on September 26, 1918, was the first mainly US battle of the war. It was a key test of the policy of US commander John Pershing in keeping his own forces separate from those of France and Britain and under his direct command. If the offensive failed, American enthusiasm for the war might be blunted, and the Germans could hope for a more favorable treaty to end the war.

The Offensive Stalls

The offensive aimed to drive the Germans away from the defenses of the Hindenburg Line. In its path lay the Argonne, a forested landscape of steep slopes and tree-covered ridges. Well-guarded river valleys, including the Meuse, pierced the forest.

About 600,000 Allied troops took part in the offensive, which

US artillery opens fire on the enemy at Meuse-Argonne. ⬇

Timeline

September 12–16, 1918
The American Expeditionary Corps, with French II Colonial Corps, attacks German-held St. Mihiel; German resistance collapses, and US troops capture 15,000 prisoners at a cost of 7,000 casualties.

September 26, 1918
The US First Army—one million men—launches the Meuse-Argonne Offensive; the first five days bring rapid gains.

September 30, 1918 The offensive halts as US troops become gridlocked on forest roads.

October 3, 1918 At the end of the first phase of the advance, two of the three German defensive lines have been taken.

October 4, 1918 The second phase of the battle begins; many US troops are veterans of the St. Mihiel battle.

(continued page 44)

August 8 France The British lead the Amiens Offensive. Many German troops flee or surrender.

September 12–16 France The American Expeditionary Corps, with a French colonial corps, captures the salient at St. Mihiel, held by the Germans since 1914.

September

September 19–21 Palestine The British defeat the Turks at the Battle of Meggido.

September 26–October 3 France One million US troops launch the Meuse-Argonne Offensive. They make rapid gains.

Timeline (continued)

October 26, 1918
The third phase of the battle begins.

October 27, 1918
Ludendorff resigns as Germany's chief military planner, clearing the way for the German government to agree to an end to the fighting with the Allies.

October 31, 1918
US forces have cleared the Argonne Forest and move into more open country; they are reorganized into two armies.

November 11, 1918 When the armistice comes into effect at 11:00 A.M., US troops are still engaged at Meuse-Argonne. They have achieved most of their goals but at a high price; the offensive has the highest death toll of any single battle in US history.

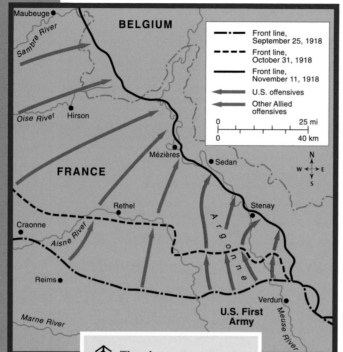

↑ The Argonne was a key point in the German defenses on the Western Front.

made good initial gains. Then things began to go wrong. The troops were too inexperienced to keep to tightly coordinated plans in such difficult terrain, and units soon fell behind. Some infantry attacks had little support and suffered heavy casualties.

Pershing tried to send in reserves but only made matters worse. The roads leading into the battle area became gridlocked. Many of the reserves could not get into battle, and some frontline units were left without supplies. By September 30, after gaining about 10 miles (16 km), the offensive had to be halted.

The Final Breakthrough

The second phase of the attack started on October 4. This time, many of the frontline troops were made up of veterans of St. Mihiel. Strong German defenses meant

Timeline
1918 October–December

October 23 Italy The Battle of Vittorio Veneto sees the Italians gain the advantage over the Austro-Hungarians.

November 1 France The final stage of the Meuse-Argonne Offensive starts; German resistance fades. Germany requests an armistice on November 6.

October — November

October 17–31 France British forces break through the German line at the Selle River.

October 29 Germany Sailors of the High Seas Fleet mutiny at their base at Kiel; other uprisings break out across Germany. The government decides to make peace before a revolution starts.

KEY:

- Western Front
- Eastern Front
- Other fronts

that progress was still slow, but the terrain often left the Americans little option other than to batter straight ahead at the enemy.

At the end of October, the US advance finally reached more open ground. The German front began to crack. By the time World War I finally came to an end on November 11, most of the US objectives had been reached. It had been a costly process, however. The 117,000 casualties were almost half of the total US losses for the whole war.

African Americans

The US Army was still segregated by color. Although African Americans made up some 13 percent of the troops in France, they were often made to do only menial support jobs. Those African Americans who reached the front line proved to be courageous fighters. Despite many instances of bravery, however, no African American was awarded the Congressional Medal of Honor.

← Parisians celebrate the armistice on November 11, 1918.

November 3 Austria-Hungary
The Austro-Hungarians seek an armistice with Italy, which is agreed to the next day.

December 1 Germany British, French, and US forces move into the Rhineland as part of the armistice terms.

December

November 9 Germany
Kaiser Wilhelm II abdicates.

November 11 Europe The armistice comes into force at 11:00 A.M.; World War I is over.

December 13 France
President Wilson arrives for the Paris peace talks—the first US president to travel abroad.

Glossary

armistice A halt in fighting agreed to by both sides

artillery Weapons for discharging missiles.

assassination A murder by sudden or secret attack often for political reasons.

blockade The isolation by a warring nation of an enemy area to prevent the passage of people or supplies.

bombard To attack with artillery.

casualty A military person lost through death, injury, sickness, or capture.

cruiser A fast, heavily armed warship.

deadlock A situation in which nothing changes.

division A military unit of between 10,000 and 20,000 troops.

dogfight A battle between two or more fighter planes.

expeditionary force Part of an army sent to fight in a foreign country.

flank The right or left wing of an army.

howitzer A type of field gun.

infantry Soldiers trained, armed, and equipped to fight on foot.

merchant ship A civilian vessel that carries cargo or passengers.

morale The emotional and spiritual strength of soldiers.

no-man's land An unoccupied area between two opposing armies.

offensive A group of military attacks.

rations Shares of food or provisions determined by supply.

salient A part of a front line that projects into enemy territory.

sector A section of a military front line.

stalemate A deadlocked position between opposing sides.

tank A tracked armored fighting vehicle.

terrain The physical features of an area of land.

trench A long cut in the ground that serves as a military defense.

ultimatum A final demand which, if not met, will lead to war.

uprising A violent rebellion against a government.

Zeppelin A long, thin, motor-powered airship.

Further Reading

Books

Adams, Simon. *World War I* (DK Eyewitness Books). DK Children, 2007.

Deary, Terry. *Frightful First World War* (Horrible Histories). Scholastic Inc, 2009.

Grant, R. G. *Why Did World War I Happen?* (Moments in History). Gareth Stevens, 2010.

Hook, Sue Vander. *The United States Enters World War I* (Essential Events). ABDO Publishing Company, 2010.

Hosch, William L. *World War I: People, Politics, and Power* (America at War). Rosen Education Service, 2009.

Kent, Zachary. *From the Lusitania to Versailles* (The United States at War). Enslow Publishers, 2011.

Peterson, Kathi Oram. *The Kid's Book of World War I: A Project and Activity Book.* Silverleaf Press, 2010.

Scherer, Glenn, and Marty Fletcher. *Primary Source Accounts of World War I.* Myreportlinks.com, 2006.

Schomp, Virginia. *World War I* (Letters from the Battlefront). Benchmark Books, 2004.

Taylor, David. *Key Battles of World War I* (20th Century Perspectives). Heinemann, 2001.

Turner, Jason. *World War I* (Great Wars Day by Day). Brown Bear Books, 2008.

Websites
www.firstworldwar.com
A multimedia history of World War I.

www.bbc.co.uk/history/worldwars/ wwone
BBC site about the war, including movies and audio galleries.

www.spartacus.schoolnet.co.uk/ FWW.htm
Spartacus Educational index to World War I for students.

www.worldwar1.com
Trenches on the website, with comprehensive reference library.

www.pbs.org/greatwar
PBS Internet companion to *The Great War and the Shaping of the 20th Century.*

www.eyewitnesstohistory.com/ w1frm.htm
Dozens of eyewitness accounts from the conflict.

Index

African Americans 45

Allies 4, 7, 12, 18, 19, 20, 21, 30, 31,35, 39, 40, 41, 42, 43

armistice 45

assassination 4, 7, 8

Ataturk 21

Australia and New Zealand Army Corps (ANZAC) 20

Battle of Arras 5

Battle of Belleau Wood 41

Battle of Cambrai 37

Battle of Flers-Courcelette 33

Battle of Jutland (Skagerrak) 22, 23, 24

Battle of Passchendaele 36

Battle of Tannenberg 14, 15, 17

Battle of the Marne 12

Battle of the Somme (Somme Offensive) 30, 31, 32, 33

Central powers 7, 17

Christmas Day 1914 truce 13

Churchill, Winston 19

convoy system 25

"Dead Man" Ridge 28

dogfights 4

Eastern Front 14, 15, 16, 17

Entente 7

Falkenhayn, General Erich von 16, 27, 29

Foch, General Ferdinand 40

Franco-Prussian War 11

Franz Ferdinand, Archduke 7, 8

Gallipoli 4, 18, 19, 20, 21

"Great War, The" 4

Haig, General Douglas 31, 33, 36

High Seas Fleet 22

Hindenburg, Field Marshal Paul von 28

Hindenburg Line 35, 43

Hötzendorf, General Franz Conrad von 15

howitzer 5, 10, 41

Jellicoe, Admiral John 23

Joffre, General Joseph 11

Kemal, Mustafa 21

Ludendorff, General Erich 28, 35, 39, 40, 41

Lusitania 4, 25

Meuse-Argonne Offensive 42, 43, 44

Nicholas II, Czar 17

Nivelle, Robert 27, 28, 36, 37

Nivelle Offensive 37

no-man's land 13, 32

North Atlantic Ocean 22, 25

North Sea 22, 23

Operation Georgette 40

Operation Michael 38, 39, 41

Ottoman Turks 18, 19, 20, 21

Pershing, John 43, 44

Pétain, General Henri-Philippe 27, 28, 29, 36

Race to the Sea 12, 13

Ravine of the Dead, The 26

Royal Navy 23

"Sacred Way, the" 29

Schlieffen, Count Alfred von 8

Schlieffen Plan 8, 9, 13

Second Battle of the Aisne 36

Serbia 8, 15, 17

stormtroopers 39, 41

submarines 4, 22, 24, 25

tanks 30, 33, 37

"They shall not pass!" 28

trenches 4, 13, 20, 21, 32

U-boats 22, 23, 24, 25

United States 4, 7, 24, 25, 41, 42, 43, 45

US Second Division 41

US Third Division 41

Verdun 26, 27, 28, 29, 31

"War to End War, The" 4

Western Front 4, 10, 13, 15, 16, 20, 26, 33, 34, 37, 40, 42, 44

Wilhelm II, Emperor 16

Wilson, President Woodrow 35

Zeppelin airships 4